DK READERS

BEGINNING
TO READ
1

Let's Play
Tennis

Written by Kate Simkins

My name is Meg.
I was really
excited today
because I had
my first
tennis lesson.

I put on my new tennis shoes and
a comfortable skirt and top.

shoes

Then I was ready to play.

A Note to Parents and Teachers

DK READERS is a compelling reading programme for beginning readers, designed in conjunction with leading literacy experts, including Cliff Moon M.Ed., Honorary Fellow of the University of Reading. Cliff Moon has spent many years as a teacher and teacher educator specializing in reading and has written more than 160 books for children and teachers. He is series editor to Collins Big Cat.

Beautiful illustrations and superb full-colour photographs combine with engaging, easy-to-read stories to offer a fresh approach to each subject in the series. Each DK READER is guaranteed to capture a child's interest while developing his or her reading skills, general knowledge and love of reading.

The five levels of DK READERS are aimed at different reading abilities, enabling you to choose the books that are exactly right for your child:

Pre-level 1: Learning to read
Level 1: Beginning to read
Level 2: Beginning to read alone
Level 3: Reading alone
Level 4: Proficient readers

The "normal" age at which a child begins to read can be anywhere from three to eight years old, so these levels are intended only as a general guideline.

No matter which level you select, you can be sure that you are helping your child learn to read, then read to learn!

LONDON, NEW YORK, MUNICH,
MELBOURNE, AND DELHI

Editor Kate Simkins
Designer Cathy Tincknell
Design Manager Lisa Lanzarini
Project Editor Lindsay Kent
Publishing Manager Simon Beecroft
Category Publisher Alex Allan
DTP Designer Hanna Ländin
Production Nick Seston

Reading Consultant
Cliff Moon, M.Ed.

First published in Great Britan in 2006 by
Dorling Kindersley Limited,
80 Strand, London WC2E 0RL
A Penguin Company

06 07 08 09 10 10 9 8 7 6 5 4 3 2 1

A CIP record for this book is available from
the British Library.

ISBN-13: 978-1-40531-513-5
ISBN-10: 1-4053-1513-X

Colour reproduction by Media Development and Printing, UK
Printed and bound by L. Rex Printing Co. Ltd, China

Discover more at
www.dk.com

I met lots of other children
at the tennis court.
They were learning
how to play tennis too.

We all shook hands with Dan,
who is our coach.

court

We had to warm ourselves up before we could begin the lesson.

We started by
marching on the spot.

marching

Then we jumped
up and down.

I circled my arms
like a windmill!

Dan showed us how
to stretch.
"Stretching stops
you hurting yourself
when you play,"
he told us.

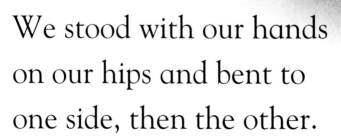

We stood with our hands
on our hips and bent to
one side, then the other.

I could feel my tummy
muscles working.

We tried bouncing a ball
on the ground and then
catching it.

I dropped my ball a few times,
but then I caught it.

Dan threw a ball to Nathan.
He had to jump up high
to catch it!

ball

racket

Dan showed us how
to hold our rackets.

My racket felt light and
easy to hold.
"I can't wait to hit a ball,"
I said excitedly.
"I want it to go a long way!"

First, we tried walking along
a line with a ball on
our tennis rackets.
It was hard to stop
the ball falling off.

"Pretend you are
walking on a tightrope,"
said Dan.

"Who wants to hit a ball?"
asked Dan.

"I do!" cried Helen.

Dan bounced
some balls and
Helen tried to hit them
with her racket.

She missed
the first few
balls, but then
she hit one.

forehand

Nathan showed us how to hit a shot called the forehand.

He held his racket in one hand
and hit the ball after it bounced.

Then I had a go.
I was really happy when
I hit the ball.

Samuel is very
good at doing
the backhand.
I watched him
hit the ball.

It went
a long way.

backhand

Dan said I could try
a backhand after
a few more lessons.
I can't wait!

Helen and I tried hitting the ball over the net before it bounced.

net

We held our rackets up high.
"Watch the ball!" called Dan.

At the end of the lesson,
Dan asked us some questions
about what we had learnt.

We got all the answers right and
Dan said we could play
some games as a reward.

Dan pretended to be
a sleeping giant.

We had to creep up on him.
If he woke up and caught us
moving, we had to start again.

He nearly caught me, but
I stopped just in time!

I had so much fun
at my first tennis lesson.
I learnt lots and made
some new friends too.

"You did really well!"
smiled Dan as we were
saying goodbye.
"See you next time!"

Picture word list

shoes
page 4

racket
page 14

court
page 7

forehand
page 20

marching
page 9

backhand
page 23

ball

page 13

net

page 24